SCIENCE ◢ SPOTLIGHT

ASTRONOMY

SCIENCE SPOTLIGHT
ASTRONOMY

IAN GRAHAM

RSVP

**RAINTREE
STECK-VAUGHN**
P U B L I S H E R S
The Steck-Vaughn Company

Austin, Texas

Published by Raintree Steck-Vaughn Publishers, an imprint of Steck-Vaughn Company

Editors: Su Swallow and Shirley Shalit
Designer: Neil Sayer
Production: Jenny Mulvanny
Electronic Production: Scott Melcer
Illustrations: Hardlines, Charlbury
Graeme Chambers

Library of Congress Cataloging-in-Publication Data

Graham, Ian, 1953-
 Astronomy / Ian Graham.
  p. cm. — (Science spotlight)
 Includes index.
 ISBN 0-8114-3841-4
 1. Astronomy — Juvenile literature. [1. Astronomy.]
 I. Title. II. Series.
 QB46.G82 1995   94-13835
 520—dc20   CIP AC

Printed in Hong Kong
Bound in the United States
1 2 3 4 5 6 7 8 9 0 LB 99 98 97 96 95 94

ACKNOWLEDGMENTS

For permission to reproduce copyright material the authors and publishers gratefully acknowledge the following:

Cover (top) NASA, Science Photo Library, (bottom) Roger Ressmeyer, Starlight, Science Photo Library **Page 4** Image Select **page 5** NASA, Science Photo Library **page 6** (top) Klaus Paysan, Image Select, (bottom) Alfred Pasieka, Science Photo Library **page 7** (main picture) Roger Ressmeyer, Science Photo Library, (bottom) Library of Congress, Science Photo Library **page 8** (top) Kent Wood, Science Photo Library, (middle) Philippe Plailly, Science Photo Library, (bottom) Roger Ressmeyer, Starlight, Science Photo Library **page 9** (middle) Image Select, (bottom left) Jisas, Lockhead, Science Photo Library **page 10** (top) NOAO, Science Photo Library, (bottom) David Parker, Science Photo Library **page 12** (top) Science Photo Library, (bottom left) Image Select, (bottom right) Roger Ressmeyer, Starlight, Science Photo Library **page 13** Ronald Royer, Science Photo Library **page 14** (top) NOAO, Science Photo Library, (bottom) Dr. Rudolph Schild, Science Photo Library **page 15** Mary Evans Picture Library **page 16** Image Select **page 17** (middle) Bryn Colton, Rex Features, (bottom) X-ray Astronomy Group, University of Leicester, Science Photo Library **page 18** (top) Image Select, (bottom) David Parker, Science Photo Library **page 19** (middle) Professor Yoshiaki Sofue, Science Photo Library, (bottom) NASA, Science Photo Library **page 20** (top) Image Select, (bottom) NASA, Science Photo Library **page 21** NASA, Science Photo Library **page 22** NASA, Science Photo Library **page 23** NASA, Science Photo Library **page 24** (top) Image Select, (bottom) NASA, Science Photo Library **page 25** (top) Novosti Press Agency, Science Photo Library, (bottom) NASA, Science Photo Library **page 26** (main picture) NASA, Science Photo Library, (inset) NASA, (bottom) Massonnet et al, CNES, Science Photo Library **page 27** (top) NASA, Science Photo Library, (bottom) Adam Hart-Davis, Science Photo Library **page 28** (top) Mary Evans Picture Library, (bottom) Science Photo Library **page 29** (top) Image Select, (middle) NASA, Science Photo Library **page 30** NASA, Science Photo Library **page 31** (top) David Hardy, Science Photo Library, (middle) NASA, Science Photo Library, (bottom) Image Select **page 32** (top) Peter Menzel, Science Photo Library, (middle) Novosti Press Agency, Science Photo Library, (bottom) Francois Gohier, Science Photo Library **page 33** (top) Pekka Parviainen, Science Photo Library, (bottom) Sinclair Stammers, Science Photo Library **page 34** David McLean, Science Photo Library **page 35** (top left) Max-Planck-Institut fur Aeronomite, David Parker, Science Photo Library, (top right) e.t. archive, (bottom) European Space Agency, Science Photo Library **page 36** (top) Mary Evans Picture Library, (bottom left) Royal Greenwich Observatory, Science Photo Library, (bottom right) Science Photo Library **page 37** Royal Observatory, Edinburgh, Science Photo Library **page 38** (top) David Hardy, Science Photo Library, (middle) Image Select, (bottom) NASA, Science Photo Library **page 39** (top) Dr. Seth Shostak, Science Photo Library, (bottom) Robin Scagell, Science Photo Library **page 40** (top) Julian Baum, Science Photo Library, (bottom) NASA GSFC, Science Photo Library **page 41** NASA, Science Photo Library **page 42** Image Select **page 43** (left) Space Telescope Science Institute, NASA, Science Photo Library, (right) Mary Evans Picture Library

CONTENTS

INTRODUCTION

Astronomy must be the oldest science of all. Long before there was any science or written history, people surely wondered why the sun rises and sets, and why the moon and stars appear to move the way they do. Their wonderings were the first steps on a journey of discovery that has lasted for thousands of years.

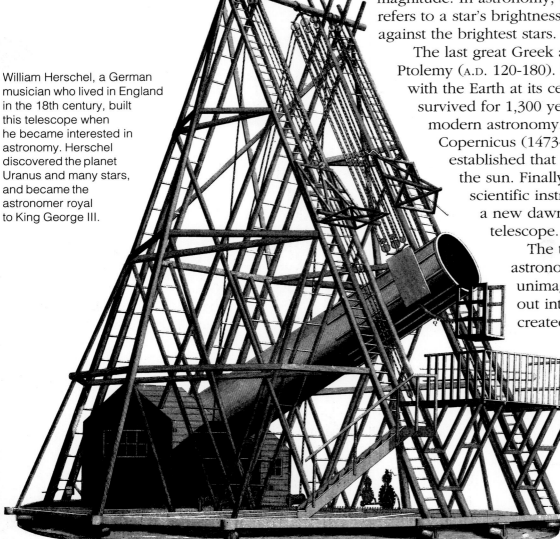

An early illustration of the Copernican system of the universe. Copernicus, a 16th-century Polish astronomer, discovered that the Earth and planets move around the sun.

William Herschel, a German musician who lived in England in the 18th century, built this telescope when he became interested in astronomy. Herschel discovered the planet Uranus and many stars, and became the astronomer royal to King George III.

The first astronomical records were made by the Chinese more than 4,500 years ago. The ancient Egyptians were clever astronomers too, but the greatest astronomers of the ancient world were the Greeks. Hipparchus invented a new kind of mathematics called trigonometry so that he could work out the positions of the stars. He managed to catalog 850 stars. He placed each of them in one of six classes according to its magnitude. In astronomy, the word magnitude refers to a star's brightness, which is measured against the brightest stars.

The last great Greek astronomer was Ptolemy (A.D. 120-180). His ideas of a universe with the Earth at its center, though wrong, survived for 1,300 years until the birth of modern astronomy. It was Nicolaus Copernicus (1473-1543) who at last established that the Earth circles the sun. Finally, in 1609 came the scientific instrument that marked a new dawn in astronomy – the telescope.

The telescope enabled astronomers to see unimaginably huge distances out into space. Astronomers created a new unit called the light-year, which is big enough to deal with the distances between stars and between galaxies (large groups of stars). Although "light-year" sounds like a length of time, it is actually a distance – the

The Hubble Space Telescope was released from a shuttle spacecraft in 1990. It is 50 times more powerful than any telescope on Earth.

The Andromeda galaxy can be seen as a faint patch of light with the naked eye. It is more than two million light-years away from our own Milky Way galaxy.

distance light travels in a year. It works out at about 5.88 trillion miles (9.46 trillion km). The closest stars to us are a few light-years away. The most distant objects in the universe that we can detect are thousands of millions of light-years away. Astronomers have developed ways of extracting an amazing amount of information from what is sometimes little more than a hazy smudge of light in the eyepiece of a telescope.

Astronomy explores some of the problems that astronomers have faced in their quest to learn more about distant planets, stars, and galaxies. **History Spotlight** boxes focus on an important technique, a piece of equipment, or a key figure in the history of

some of the topics. Key words are explained in the glossary on page 44.

TEMPERATURES

Temperature is measured on a scale of degrees. There are different scales. On the Fahrenheit scale, water freezes at 32° (0°C) and boils at 212° (100°C). Scientists also use the kelvin scale, named after the physicist Lord Kelvin. On this scale zero degrees kelvin is the same as -459° Fahrenheit (-273°C). Both scales are used in this book. Where 100 degrees is written, it means 100 degrees kelvin.

INSIDE THE FIREBALL

The sun is a star that rises every day without fail. It gives the Earth life by providing the light and warmth that plants and animals need. For centuries, scientists have tried to discover what makes this fireball shine. Finally, at the beginning of the 20th century, a German scientist named Albert Einstein gave scientists a clue to what might be happening inside stars like the sun.

Life on Earth depends on the sun for light and warmth.

Warning: Never look directly at the sun, even through dark glasses, and never ever through binoculars or a telescope, or you may permanently damage your eyes.

The sun has been pouring out a huge amount of energy for billions of years. Scientists knew this from the fossil remains of plants and animals – they could not have existed without the sun and they could be dated to millions of years ago. The sun looks like a burning ball, but scientists knew that it could not simply be burning. If it was burning in the same way that coal or wood burns, it would have used up all of its fuel after a few thousand years. It must be using some other way of producing light and heat.

One of the basic laws of nature, called the law of conservation of energy, states that energy can never be created or destroyed, it can only be changed from one form into another. So, the sun must be changing energy already stored inside it into light and heat. In the 19th century, scientists tried to solve this puzzle by thinking about what might happen if the sun became smaller. If the atoms in the outermost layers of the sun were pulled in toward the center by the sun's own force of gravity, they would become packed more closely together and crash into each other more often. The temperature of the outer layer would rise. Some of the gravity energy absorbed by the atoms would escape again as light and heat. If this theory was correct, it would mean that the sun must have been shrinking in size throughout all of its life. Could this be true? The two scientists who developed the theory calculated that if the sun had contracted by only 130 feet (40 m) every year, it would produce just the right amount of light and heat for about 100 million years. The puzzle seemed to have been solved when, at the beginning of the 20th century, geologists calculated that the Earth must be at least several *billion* (thousand million) years old. The Earth is only here because the sun exists, so the sun must be at least several billion years old, too. According to the shrinking sun theory, the sun should therefore be

Fossils provided scientists with some of the first real clues to the sun's age. These fossil insects in a piece of amber are about 40 million years old.

much smaller than it is today so this theory had to be wrong, after all. At about the same time, Einstein developed a theory that suggested that it was possible for matter, the stuff that everything is made of, to change into energy. Einstein expressed this by one of the most famous scientific equations of all:

$$E = mc^2$$ or energy = mass x speed of light x speed of light.

Energy and matter are equivalent. They are merely two different forms of the same thing. And, because the speed of light is a huge number —186,000 miles (300,000 km) per second — a tiny piece of matter is equivalent to a huge amount of energy. But how could the sun be changing into energy? And if the sun's matter has been fading for billions of years, why has it not completely disappeared by now?

Scientists calculated that about four and a half million tons of matter would have to be converted to energy every second to produce the light and heat that we receive from the sun! That is a huge amount of matter to lose every

Albert Einstein and his wife moved to America in 1930.

A total eclipse of the sun allows astronomers to study the outer regions of the sun. These are normally invisible because of the very bright light of the inner region.

A Solar Telescope

The McMath solar telescope is the largest telescope in the world for studying the sun. It stands at Kitt Peak National Observatory in Arizona. The support tower (right) is about 109 feet (33 m) high. The tracking mirror at the top (below), which follows the path of the sun, reflects sunlight down a diagonal tunnel that reaches deep underground. (See artwork below.)

An astronomer measures sunspots in the observing room of the McMath telescope. He wears dark glasses to protect his eyes from the intense light.

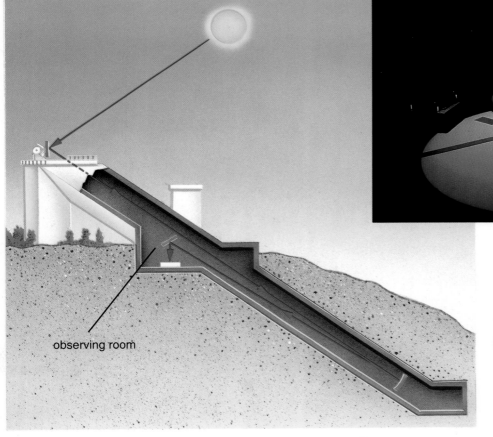

observing room

In the McMath solar telescope, a mirror at the top of the tower catches sunlight and sends it underground to another mirror, which sends the light beam up to an observing room.

Most of the telescope is underground to keep it cool. A change in temperature would affect the delicate measuring instruments.

second, but the sun is so massive that it could lose matter at that rate for 10 billion years before running out of fuel. Scientists have estimated that the sun has been shining for about four and a half billion years, so it is about halfway through its life span.

NUCLEAR FUSION

What is the fuel of the sun? The sun was known to be composed mainly of hydrogen, the lightest element of all. At the center of the sun, the temperature is an incredible 15 million degrees. At this temperature, particles of matter are racing around at very high speeds, about 600 miles (1,000 km) per second. At these speeds, collisions between particles are common and so violent that sometimes the particles stick together. This is called nuclear fusion. As all the particles involved in these collisions are common in the universe and therefore common on Earth too, scientists have been able to measure their mass. They found that the final clump of fused particles contains less matter than the individual particles. The mass that disappears when the particles fuse together is changed into energy. Scientists have calculated that if about two pounds (1 kg.) of matter could be converted into energy, it would produce the same amount of energy as all the electricity, coal, oil, and gas used everywhere on Earth for ten years. Ten years of energy for the whole world from a lump of matter small enough to hold in your hand! Not surprisingly, scientists have been trying for decades to copy the sun's energy factory on Earth, but so far, fusion energy has proved to be too difficult to produce commercially.

A 19th-century illustration of solar prominences, gas flares that can be several hundred thousand miles long!

An image of the sun made from X-ray data collected by a Japanese satellite in 1991.

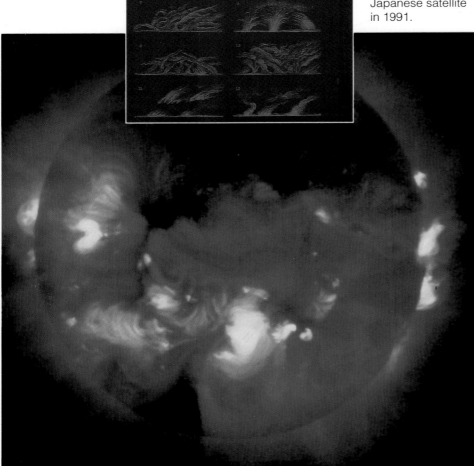

HISTORY / SPOTLIGHT

Scientists in the former Soviet Union were the first to build experimental fusion reactors. Their reactor, called a tokamak, has been improved on by scientists in the United States and England. In 1988, the hydrogen fuel inside the Joint European Torus, a tokamak in England, reached a temperature of 100 million degrees — an important milestone in fusion research. The fuel is so hot that it would melt any container, so it is held in place, away from the walls, by complicated magnetic fields. Nuclear fusion is very difficult to achieve, and a working fusion reactor capable of generating electrical power is probably still decades away.

Scientists checking the inside of an American tokamak fusion reactor.

POINTS OF LIGHT

Many early astronomers believed that stars are so far away that we would never know anything about them. In fact, astronomers can now tell how far away a star is, what it is made from, and how hot it is simply by looking at it and analyzing the light and other energy that reaches us from it.

A cluster of stars about 400 light-years away.

A beam of white light passes through a glass prism and forms a spectrum.

If you look at the night sky for a while, you will notice that some stars are reddish and others are bluish. Scientific instruments can detect many more differences between the light from different stars. In 1815, Bavarian scientist Joseph von Fraunhofer noticed that when he used a wedge of glass called a prism to spread out the light from a star into the rainbow of colors the light contains, there were black lines running between the colored bands. Once scientists understood the black lines, they could work out what a star is made from, how hot it is, and how far away it is.

If a single chemical element is heated until it glows or burns and the light from it is spread out by a prism, it does not produce a rainbow. Instead, there are just a few colored lines. Each element produces its own unique group of lines. Elements not only *produce* light in this special way, they also absorb it. If light shines through a cloud of gas, the gas absorbs some of the light, leaving black gaps in the spectrum of the background light. In the same way, when light from the deep hot layers of a star shines through its gassy atmosphere, some of it is absorbed. By analyzing which colors are missing from the star's rainbow spectrum, scientists can tell which elements are present in the star's atmosphere.

Scientists can also tell how hot the star is, because the strength of the colors on the spectrum depends on the star's surface temperature. For example, the colors produced by hydrogen are strongest at a temperature of about 10,000 degrees. Depending on the color of a star and the appearance of its spectrum, astronomers can place it in one of seven different temperature bands, called spectral classes. They range from red stars at less than 3,500 degrees through orange, yellow, white, blue/white, blue, and finally violet stars. The temperature of violet stars is more than 25,000 degrees.

A Star's Spectrum

When light from a star passes through a prism, it separates into a spectrum of colors. Chemical elements in a star's atmosphere absorb some of the colors, leaving black "absorption" lines in the spectrum. Each element creates its own pattern of black spectral lines, so astronomers can use them to work out what elements a star's atmosphere contains.

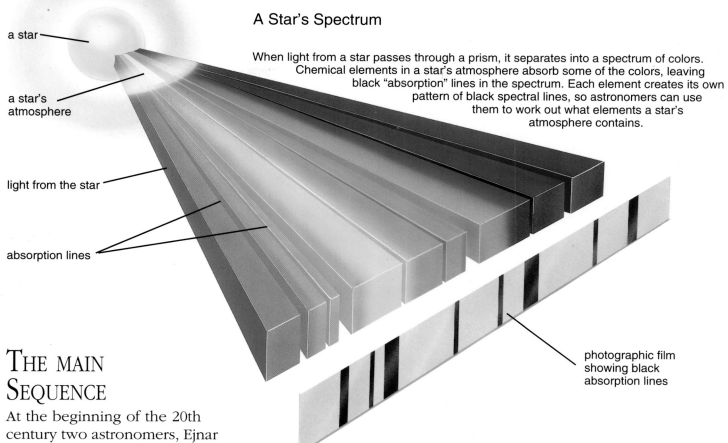

a star

a star's atmosphere

light from the star

absorption lines

photographic film showing black absorption lines

THE MAIN SEQUENCE

At the beginning of the 20th century two astronomers, Ejnar Hertzsprung and Henry Norris Russell, started noting down stars whose distances were already known, together with their magnitude (brightness – see page 4). When the distances were plotted on a graph, most of the stars were grouped together along a line — from hot bright stars at the top left to cool dim stars at the bottom right. This band of stars is called the main sequence. The graph, called the Hertzsprung-Russell diagram or H-R diagram, gives astronomers a way of estimating how far away a star is. When a star's temperature and magnitude are plotted on the H-R diagram, its actual brightness can also be read off the diagram. To estimate distance, it is also essential to know how big the star is, because a bigger, brighter star far away could look as bright as a small star closer to

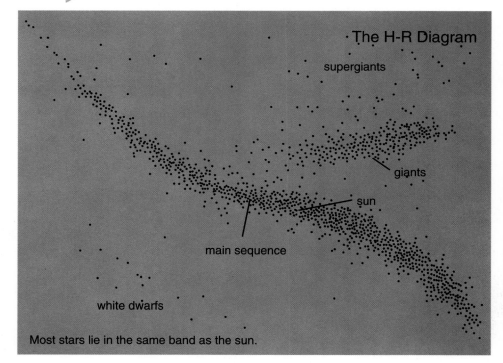

The H-R Diagram

supergiants

giants

sun

main sequence

white dwarfs

Most stars lie in the same band as the sun.

us. Bigger stars have a stronger force of gravity which compresses their core more than smaller stars. These differences in pressure leave telltale signs in the star's

spectrum that astronomers can recognize. Knowing how big a star is, how bright it is, and how much less bright it looks from Earth, astronomers can calculate how far away it must be.

ISLAND UNIVERSES

When astronomers first used telescopes, in the 17th century, they saw faint fuzzy patches of light that looked like clouds. The patches were named after the Latin word for clouds, *nebulae*. When the distances between Earth and some of these nebulae were calculated, it changed forever our view of the universe.

By the beginning of the 20th century, astronomers had found over 15,000 nebulae. Some of them really were clouds (of gas), but when others were observed through powerful telescopes astronomers could see stars inside them. These nebulae were actually clusters of stars – galaxies. Astronomers noticed that some of the stars in some nebulae rose and fell in brightness in a regular and rhythmic way. In 1924 the American astronomer Edwin Hubble discovered that these variable stars were a type of star called a cepheid variable. All the other known cepheid variables were supergiant stars about 10,000 times brighter than the sun. This meant that the variable stars in these nebulae must also be supergiants. Yet they looked small and faint from Earth. The answer must be that we are seeing them from an enormous distance.

HOW FAR TO THE GALAXIES?

One way to measure the distance to faraway galaxies relies on the fact that most galaxies spin. All galaxies contain clouds of hydrogen gas.

Edwin Hubble, the American astronomer whose work proved the existence of galaxies outside our own.

The Lick Observatory in California, the first permanent mountaintop observatory in the world, houses early telescopes (inset) and modern ones. It has provided excellent seeing conditions, but air pollution is now beginning to interfere with results.

A view of the center of the Milky Way galaxy, taken from Australia.

These clouds of hydrogen send out radio waves with a wavelength of about eight and a half inches (21 cm). As the galaxy rotates, the hydrogen on one side of the galaxy comes toward us and the hydrogen on the other side of the galaxy rushes away from us. How do astronomers make use of this? Imagine an airplane flying toward you. As it gets closer, the frequency (pitch) of its engine noise rises. Each time a sound wave leaves the engines, the airplane has flown a little closer to you. The waves reach you closer and closer together, which the ear hears as a rising pitch. This is known as the Doppler effect, named after the Austrian scientist who discovered it. It works in the opposite way when the airplane is flying away from you.

A rotating galaxy produces a Doppler effect too, spreading out the eight-and-a half inch hydrogen radio signal from a single wavelength to a broader band of wavelengths. The wider the band is, the faster the galaxy must be spinning. Once astronomers know how fast a galaxy is spinning, they can work out how big it is. The more slowly a galaxy spins, the bigger it is. The bigger it is, the more stars it contains. And the more stars it contains, the brighter it is. So, there is a link between how fast a galaxy spins and how bright it is. By comparing its actual brightness with how bright it looks from Earth, astronomers can estimate how far away it is.

Our galaxy, the Milky Way, is a spiral of 100 billion stars 100,000 light-years across cartwheeling through space. The stars lie in a flattened disk about 2,000 light-years thick with a bulge about 10,000 light-years thick in the middle. The sun lies about two thirds of the way out from the center along one of the spiral arms. It orbits the center of the galaxy at about 150 miles (250 km) per second. Even at this great speed, it takes 250 million years for each complete orbit.

The Milky Way

Our sun (shown as a red dot) lies on the edge of one of the main spiral arms of the galaxy (top). The side view (above) shows the bulge in the center of the galaxy.

STAR DEATH

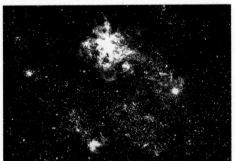

Before and after: the top picture shows stars in a nearby galaxy in 1969. The bottom picture was taken in 1987, just after one of the stars had exploded. Supernova 1987A is the bright star on the right.

The Crab Nebula, with a neutron star at its center, is the remains of a supernova explosion that was observed by Chinese astronomers in 1054.

Stars do not last forever. Eventually their fuel is used up and the balance of forces inside them changes, sometimes violently. Astronomers now know what happens to a star at the end of its life. Some simply fade away, while others explode in a huge fireball.

The more massive a star is, the more violent its end. But most stars will end their days in the same way as our own sun. In about another five billion years, the sun will have converted most of the hydrogen in its core to helium by nuclear fusion (see page 9). As the core gradually changes from hydrogen to heavier helium, the pressure increases and it heats up, making the star shine more brightly. Eventually, there is no hydrogen left in the core and nuclear fusion comes to a halt.

Up to this point, the inward force of gravity trying to make the star collapse has been balanced by an equal outward force caused by the intense heat of the nuclear activity in its core. Although fusion ceases in the star's core, it continues in a shell outside it. More and more helium is dumped into the core until it cannot support its own weight and it collapses. The collapse itself generates heat, which makes the outer layers expand. The surface expands so much that it cools to a dull red color, giving the star its name – a red giant. When this happens to the sun, it will grow so large that it will swallow up Mercury, Venus, and Earth. Anything living on Earth at that time will be vaporized.

The outer layers of a dying star eventually expand out into space, leaving behind a small, cool star called a white dwarf. This cools down and finally disappears from view.

THE DEMISE OF THE HEAVYWEIGHTS

Astronomers believe that quite a different fate awaits stars that are more than 12 times the mass of the sun. The core of a "heavyweight" collapses suddenly. It can go from the size of the Earth to between 6 and 60 miles (10 and 100 km) across in less than a second! The shock of this sudden collapse is so violent that it blows the outer layers of the star away in a giant explosion called a supernova.

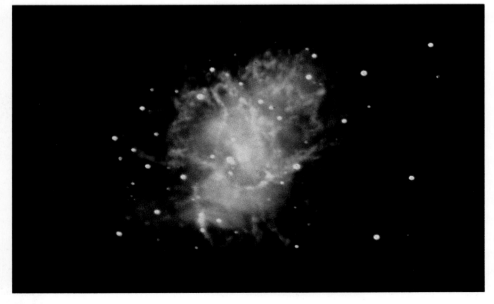

The brightest supernovae are clearly visible to the naked eye. Astronomers have estimated that they must be 10 billion times brighter than the sun. They do not stay this bright for very long. As the shell of material is blown away into space, it expands, cools, loses its brightness, and fades away after a few months. The collapsed core is incredibly dense, so dense that elements and chemical compounds as we know them cannot exist. The dying star is composed almost entirely of particles called neutrons. It is therefore called a neutron star. Because so much matter is compressed into such a small volume, the force of gravity at the star's surface is enormous, perhaps 100,000 million times the force of gravity on Earth.

The collapse that forms a neutron star is so sudden that the neutron star spins very quickly – as fast as 1,000 times per second! Particles escaping from the star's surface are caught up in the intense magnetic field that surrounds it. They give out radio waves which are squeezed by the field into two beams. As the star spins, the radio beams sweep around the sky like beams of light from a lighthouse. Astronomers can detect them on Earth. The rate at which the star blinks on and off at radio wavelengths shows how quickly it is spinning.

STARDUST

The particles shot into space by a supernova spread throughout the galaxy. Many of them are swept up by other stars, sucked in by the star's force of gravity. Others are trapped by clouds of matter and, after millions of years, form new stars. We have reason to be grateful that some stars explode in this way, because we, and everything around us in the solar system, are composed of atoms made in stars that have blown themselves to bits. We are literally made from the dust of stars.

A Lighthouse in the Sky

Radio waves from a neutron star are picked up as a ticking sound on a radio telescope every time the beam sweeps across the Earth.

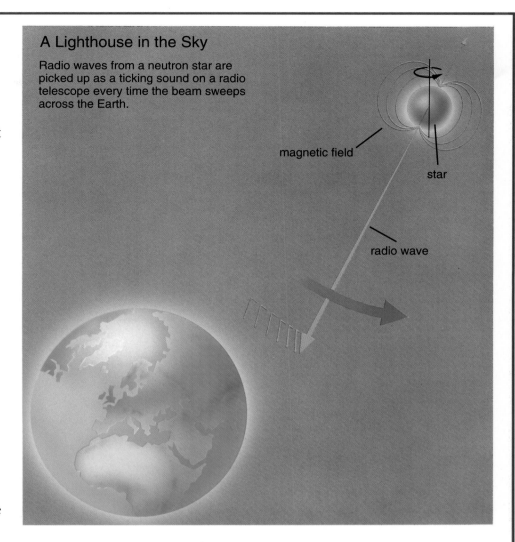

magnetic field

star

radio wave

A 19th-century image of astronomers in ancient China.

BLACK STARS

Some stars are invisible. They are as black as the space around them. Scientific theories predicted that there should be stars so massive that nothing, not even light, could escape their enormous pull of gravity. Astronomers have found evidence for them. But how do you set about looking for something that is invisible? And how do you know when you have found it?

Gravity pulls this spent fuel tank, dropped from a rocket, back to Earth. Some objects have such a powerful pull of gravity that nothing, not even light, can escape from them.

The theories developed by astronomers to describe what happens inside a star and to predict how stars die pointed to an astonishing fate for the most massive stars. It seemed too fantastic to be true. Every star has a strong force of gravity. The sun's gravity holds the solar system together. The Earth has a force of gravity, too. If you throw a ball up into the air, gravity pulls it back down again. If you could throw it fast enough, it might overcome the force of gravity and fly out into space. The speed that something needs to break free from a planet (or a star) is called the escape velocity. Earth's escape velocity is about 24,000 miles per hour, or 6.6 miles (11 km) per second. Stars are much more massive than planets (the sun is 333,000 times the mass of the Earth) and so they have much stronger gravitational forces than planets. The escape velocity of the sun is therefore much higher than that of the Earth – it is 370 miles (618 km) per second, or more than a million miles per hour!

It is possible to imagine a star so massive and with such a huge force of gravity that its escape velocity would be greater than the speed of light. As nothing can travel faster than light, nothing could ever leave the surface of the star, not even light itself. It would be an invisible star, a black star, or a black hole, as these incredible objects have become known.

LOOKING FOR BLACK HOLES

If light cannot leave a black hole, then it can never be seen. The idea of an invisible star is very difficult to believe, but once the theory had predicted them astronomers had to find a way of looking for them. Even though a black hole itself cannot be seen, its effects on nearby stars and matter in general might be detectable. Gas or dust near a black hole would fall toward it and eventually be sucked inside. As a cloud of gas or dust moved toward the black

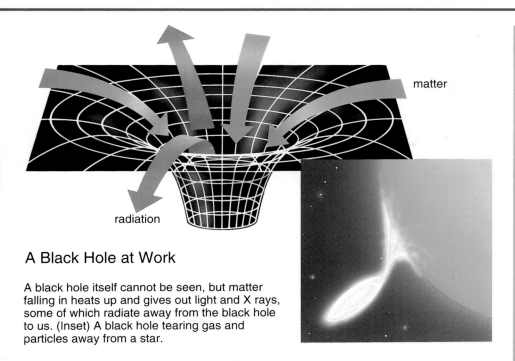

A Black Hole at Work

A black hole itself cannot be seen, but matter falling in heats up and gives out light and X rays, some of which radiate away from the black hole to us. (Inset) A black hole tearing gas and particles away from a star.

HISTORY SPOTLIGHT

The black hole seems to be a very modern idea, predicted by modern theories, but in fact some astronomers had wondered if such an object might have existed hundreds of years ago. As long ago as 1783, John Michell, a professor at Cambridge University, England, wondered about the possibility of a star whose escape velocity was greater than the speed of light. The name "black hole" was coined more recently by the American scientist John Wheeler in 1969, although the French mathematician Pierre Simon, the Marquis de Laplace, had written about black stars that he called dark bodies in 1796.

Stephen Hawking has researched black holes since the 1960s.

hole, it would start to spin. Just before it disappeared, it would be traveling so fast that collisions between the atoms would heat up the cloud to such a high temperature that it would give out X rays.

It was clear that astronomers would have to search the sky for X-ray sources that might be black holes. But X rays are blocked by the Earth's atmosphere. The search had to wait until the dawn of the space age, when X-ray telescopes could be taken above the atmosphere into space. One of the first X-ray sources found was Cygnus X-1. It seems to be a good candidate for a black hole. It appears to be a strong source of X rays coming from a tiny volume, possibly a collapsed star. But black holes are not the only sort of collapsed stars that could emit X rays. Neutron stars can be strong X-ray sources too. So, is Cygnus X-1 really a black hole or is it a neutron star?

Other possible black holes have also been found. As the

idea of the black hole has become more acceptable to astronomers, more possibilities for their existence have been suggested (see pages 18-19). Black holes may be very common in the universe, but their existence has not been definitely proved.

Engineers at work on the European Exosat X-ray satellite.

Radio astronomy began by accident! In 1931 Karl Jansky, working for the Bell Telephone Laboratories in New Jersey, built an aerial to investigate radio interference – hisses and crackles. He found that the crackling noises were caused by faraway storms, but the hissing noise came from space. A few years later, an astronomer built a dish-shaped aerial which detected radio energy coming from many points in the sky. The new science of radio astronomy was born.

Karl Jansky with his radio aerial system.

A modern radio telescope, which picks up radio waves from space and relays them to the "focus point" at the top of the central tower. From there, the signal is fed to the telescope's computers.

RADIO STARS

In the early 1960s, astronomers found that some stars were sending out a lot of radio energy, which was very unusual. When their light was analyzed, they were found to be much too far away to be stars. When scientists finally unraveled the story behind these strange objects, it provided evidence for black holes.

The key to understanding these starlike objects came when astronomers noticed something odd about their spectra. When the light from one of these strong radio sources was spread out into a spectrum, the lines crossing it (see pages 10-11) looked like a well-known pattern of lines produced by hydrogen, but they were in the wrong place. Instead of being at the blue end of the spectrum, they appeared to have been shifted all the way along to the red end. Astronomers already knew that the galaxies are rushing away from us at great speeds and because of this they have "red-shifted" spectra. It is another example of the Doppler effect at work (see page 13). The galaxies are flying away from us so quickly that their light waves become stretched and look longer (redder) to us than they really are.

The size of the red shift is a measure of how far away the galaxy is. The mysterious radio sources had such huge red shifts that they could not possibly be nearby stars. They had to be much farther away. They were small objects that somehow managed to shine more brightly than a galaxy. Astronomers called them quasi-stellar objects, but they are better known as quasars.

Astronomers calculated that a quasar no bigger than our solar system is as bright as the whole Milky Way galaxy, which is many millions of times larger. The question that all astronomers wanted to answer was – how does a quasar manage to generate such a huge amount of energy from such a tiny volume of space? Could it be a black hole?

THE MILKY WAY –
A QUIET QUASAR?

At first, quasars seemed quite unlike any other galaxy, especially "quiet" galaxies like our own. Since then, more galaxies have been found with very active centers. "Active" galaxies, as they are known, all have very small yet very bright centers, indicating a great outpouring of energy and possibly the presence of a black hole. Our own Milky Way galaxy also has lots of stars near its center. In fact, there are so many stars and so much gas and dust that we cannot see the center of the galaxy. Light cannot get through to us, but the most energetic radiations such as X rays and gamma rays do manage to punch their way through. Astronomers have tried to build a picture of what is happening at the center of the galaxy by using these radiations. They have found that clouds of gas appear to be revolving around the center and falling in toward it. There seems to be a sharp boundary between the ring of gas clouds and a relatively empty space inside it, possibly caused by a massive explosion at or near the center of the galaxy. The mass needed to keep the gas clouds in orbit around the center has been calculated to be two to five million times the mass of the sun.

Such a great mass in a small space could be a black hole, but it is not conclusive proof that there is a black hole at the center of our galaxy. It could be a neutron star, but if it could be shown that the two to five million solar masses of matter were concentrated into an object roughly the same size as our sun (about 865,000 miles — 1.4 million km — across), the evidence for a black hole would be very strong indeed. And there is some evidence for this. Strong radio signals have been traced back to an object about 900 million miles (1,500 million km) across at the center of the galaxy. This could be energy radiating back from a black hole or it could be energy radiating back from a neutron star. This is one detective story that has not yet been solved by astronomers.

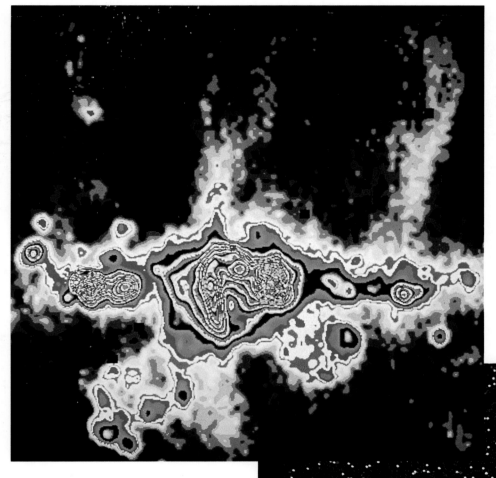

A map of the center of our galaxy recorded by a radio telescope in Japan.

An X-ray image of the first quasar to be found, in the 1960s. It is the nearest quasar to us, about 2,100 million light-years away from Earth.

THE SOLAR SYSTEM

We now know that the solar system contains nine planets, but people were not always aware of this. Until powerful telescopes were developed, people knew only the first five planets that could be seen easily – Mercury, Venus, Mars, Jupiter, and Saturn. But as astronomers began to understand more about the way the planets moved, they could tell that something was not quite right. And this gave them a clue that there might be more planets. But how many more and where were they?

Neptune's moon Triton, which orbits in the opposite direction to every other large body in the solar system.

The first sign that there might be more than the five well-known planets came in 1781. Using a telescope that he had made himself, William Herschel began making a systematic survey of the heavens (see page 4). Within a month, he had discovered an object that did not appear to be a star or any known planet.

Uranus (the blue planet) and its moons. It has no heat source to provide the energy to drive stormy weather systems, so it looks featureless.

Herschel mistakenly identified it as a comet. Mathematicians followed the new object's movement and soon discovered that it was not moving as they would expect a comet to move. Once it was known to be a planet, which was named Uranus, astronomers searched for any evidence of moons around it. Herschel himself discovered three, which were named Titania, Oberon, and Umbriel.

By 1790, astronomers had used the movements of Uranus to predict its orbit around the sun. But the planet refused to follow its predicted path. It was eventually realized that Uranus was straying from its calculated orbit because another unknown planet was pulling on it. Finally, on September 23, 1846, two astronomers working at the Berlin Observatory found a

1	Sun	6	Jupiter
2	Mercury	7	Saturn
3	Venus	8	Uranus
4	Earth	9	Neptune
5	Mars	10	Pluto

"star" which did not appear on the latest star chart. On the following night, the object had moved compared to the surrounding stars, proving that it was indeed a planet. It was named Neptune.

The discovery of Neptune did not completely explain the difference between Uranus's predicted orbit and its actual orbit. In fact, Neptune itself was straying from its predicted orbit. The answer was that yet another planet was pulling both Uranus and Neptune out of orbit.

PLANET SPOTTING

In the late 1920s, an American astronomer called Clyde Tombaugh was invited to the Lowell Observatory at Flagstaff, Arizona, to search for this elusive planet. Tombaugh conducted his search by taking two photographs of a small part of the sky a few nights apart and checking to see if anything in the pictures had moved.

In 1930 Tombaugh found a speck that seemed to be moving. This turned out to be the missing planet, later named Pluto. For most of the time, Pluto orbits the sun farther out than Neptune. But for about 20 years of its 248-year orbit, it crosses inside Neptune's orbit.

This image of Neptune reveals the Great Dark Spot, which is a giant storm the size of the Earth. Winds of 400 mph (650 kph) blow clouds of frozen methane around the planet.

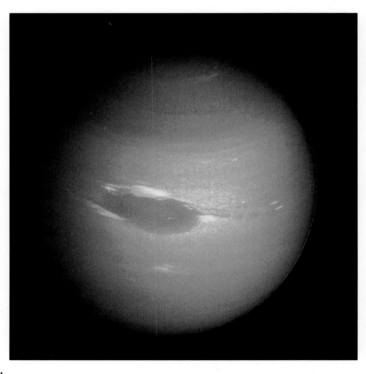

MOON QUEST

Scientists have always wanted to answer two questions about the moon – where did it come from and does it have a molten core like the Earth?

It was impossible to study the moon's structure and geology until the space age. Then spacecraft were sent to orbit the moon and take measurements of, for example, its magnetic field. Later, astronauts visited the moon. They carried out scientific experiments on the moon's surface and left instruments that continued to work after they left.

Some of the *Apollo* experiments monitored ground tremors. These "moonquakes" were much weaker than earthquakes and occurred much deeper underground. This suggested to the scientists that the moon is more solid than the Earth. Other experiments worked by setting off small explosions on the surface and listening for any reflections bouncing back from the underground layers. Sensors on one side of the moon detected vibrations on the other side that provided information about the moon's center. The results suggest that the moon is solid rock, with a small molten iron core.

The launch of the *Apollo 11* in 1969, the first manned mission to the moon.

A sample of lunar rock. Astronauts brought back nearly 880 pounds (400 kg) of rock samples to Earth.

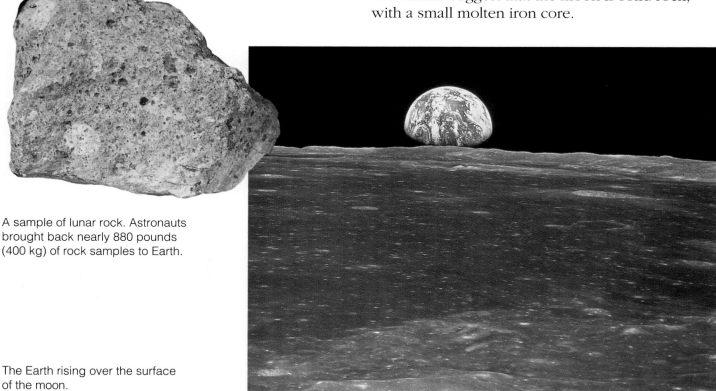

The Earth rising over the surface of the moon.

IN THE BEGINNING

The Earth could have acquired its only moon in one of three ways. The moon and Earth could have been formed at the same time from the same cloud of debris, but for some reason they did not come together to form a single body. Secondly, the moon could have come from somewhere else in the solar system and become captured by the Earth's gravitational field. Finally, it could actually be part of the Earth that was torn away.

The capture theory is perhaps the easiest of the three to imagine, but to a scientist it is the most improbable. If the moon had flown close enough to the Earth to be captured, it would have gone into a very elongated, elliptical orbit. But the moon actually has an almost circular orbit.

When moon rocks brought back to earth by the *Apollo* astronauts were examined, they were very similar to the sort of rock that is found in the Earth's crust. This also makes it unlikely that the moon and Earth formed in different parts of the galaxy and came together later. They are too alike. They must have been formed close together in space.

Although moon rocks and Earth rocks are similar, there are enough differences between them to suggest that the moon and Earth were not both formed from exactly the same material. Scientists also calculated that it would be impossible for part of the Earth to split away and form the moon all on its own. That seems to defeat all three theories! However, a combination of two of these theories seems to explain all the evidence satisfactorily.

A CHIP OFF THE OLD BLOCK!

If the Earth was struck a glancing blow by an object the size of Mars, it could just about survive without shattering into a million pieces. Material mostly from the outer layers of the Earth and the other body would be flung into space. In time, this material would condense into the ball of matter that we know as the moon. As the moon would contain rocky material from the Earth, this would account for similarities between Earth rocks and moon rocks. But the moon would also contain a lot of rocky material from the other body, which is why Earth rocks and moon rocks are similar but not identical. If the theory is correct, the moon could literally be a "chip off the old block" of Mother Earth!

HISTORY SPOTLIGHT

Neil Armstrong and Edwin "Buzz" Aldrin were the first people to land on the moon. Their *Apollo 11* lunar module touched down on July 20, 1969, while Michael Collins continued to circle the moon in the command module. The following day, Neil Armstrong became the first person to step on the moon, followed soon by Aldrin. All three astronauts returned safely to Earth in the command module on July 24.

The crew of *Apollo 11* are welcomed to Chicago after their historic mission.

Exploring the moon in the rover vehicle.

THE GREENHOUSE PLANET

Scientists learn about the planets by studying their surface features. But how do you study the surface of a planet that you cannot see? Venus is permanently covered by a thick atmosphere. Yet scientists have found a way to make detailed maps of the planet's invisible surface.

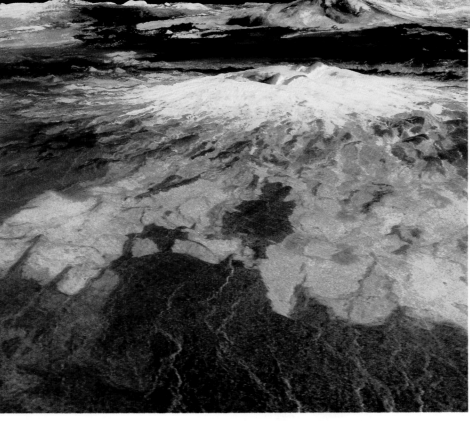

A view of Venus (right), put together from a series of photographs taken by the *Magellan* spacecraft, which also provided the information for the computer image (below) of one of the planet's huge volcanoes.

Venus is very similar in size to the Earth, but its atmosphere is completely different. The Earth's atmosphere contains a very small amount of carbon dioxide – only about 0.05 percent. The atmosphere around Venus is 96 percent carbon dioxide. It traps so much heat from the sun that there is no water on the surface anymore. It has all evaporated. And volcanoes pump so much sulfur dioxide into the atmosphere that it forms clouds of sulfuric acid that completely cover the planet. Venus is an example of the greenhouse effect gone mad. This caused one major problem for scientists who wanted to study Venus – they could not see its surface.

Pictures of Venus taken by the Russian *Venera* spacecraft.

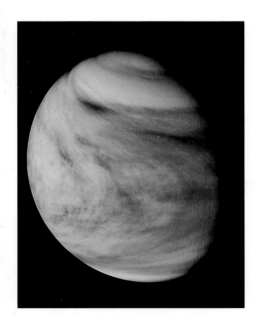

A *Pioneer-Venus* photograph showing the planet's yellow-white cloud cover.

SEEING THE INVISIBLE

In order to learn more about Venus, scientists had to find a way of seeing the surface. Although light cannot penetrate the thick acid clouds, other radiations can. Radio waves pass straight through the clouds as if they were not there, so radar was chosen as the best way of probing the Venusian surface. The former Soviet Union obtained the first photographs of the planet's surface. Its *Venera 9* and *10* spacecraft landed on Venus in 1975 and sent photographs of the surface by radio to mother-craft orbiting the planet. These craft relayed the pictures to Earth. Getting a spacecraft onto the surface in good working order was a remarkable achievement, because Venus is an extremely hostile place. Apart from sulfuric acid clouds, the surface temperature roasts any visiting spacecraft at more than 842°F (450°C) and an atmospheric pressure 100 times the air pressure on Earth does its very best to crush the craft.

Serious attempts to map the surface began with the American *Pioneer-Venus* probes in the 1970s. *Pioneer-Venus 1* fired radar pulses at Venus as it orbited the planet. The time taken for them to travel from the spacecraft down to the planet's surface and back up to the spacecraft depended on the distance between the spacecraft and the mountains, hills, and hollows on the surface. The return times for the radar pulses could be turned into a map of the Venusian surface. The map showed that almost two-thirds of the planet's surface is flat. There are two raised "continents" called Aphrodite and Ishtar. The highest point on Venus was found to be a mountain range on Ishtar rising to 36,300 feet (11,000 m), compared to 29,248 feet (8,863 m) for the Earth's highest peak, Mount Everest.

In 1989 NASA sent a new radar mapper to Venus. The spacecraft *Magellan* carried a new type of radar system called synthetic aperture radar, to create a very detailed map of Venus. A radar system with a large antenna (to transmit and receive the radar pulses) "sees" finer detail than a radar system with a small antenna. Synthetic aperture radar is a way of tricking a radar system with a small antenna into behaving like a system with a larger antenna. It can make a map with finer detail than the system should really be capable of. In fact, to record surface detail as fine as *Magellan* achieved, a single antenna 5,280 feet (1,600 m) long would have been needed! Using synthetic aperture radar, *Magellan* managed the same performance with an antenna only 11.8 feet

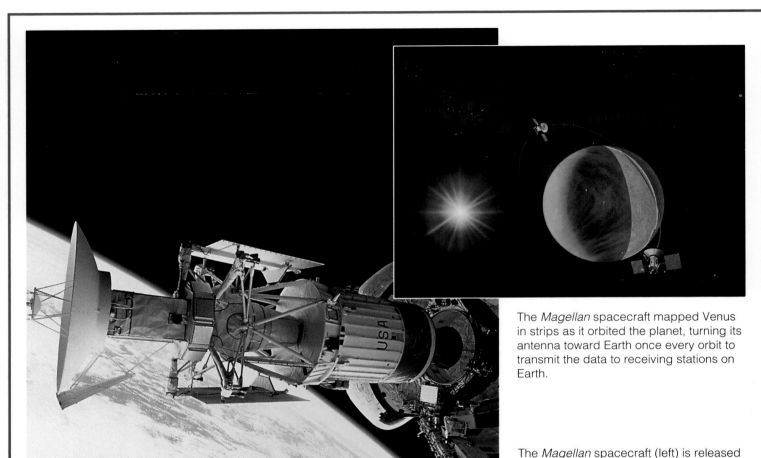

The *Magellan* spacecraft mapped Venus in strips as it orbited the planet, turning its antenna toward Earth once every orbit to transmit the data to receiving stations on Earth.

The *Magellan* spacecraft (left) is released from a space shuttle and heads for Venus.

(3.6 m) long. The smallest feature that could be seen by *Pioneer-Venus 1* was the size of the city of Los Angeles. The Soviet probes, *Venera 15* and *16*, improved on this. But the spacecraft *Magellan* could "see" surface features as small as 330 feet (100 m) across and measure the height of the surface at any point to within 165 feet (50 m).

RADAR TRICKERY

As *Magellan* traveled along its orbital path, it fired radar pulses down at the planet's surface. Each time the spacecraft's elongated, elliptical orbit brought it close to the planet, the radar recorded data from a 9,600-mile (16,000-km) long strip only 14 miles (24 km) wide. The strip observed on each pass overlapped the previous one, because by the time the spacecraft returned to the planet on its next orbit for a mapping pass, the planet had turned slowly, presenting a new strip of the surface to the instruments. Nothing out of the ordinary so far – but the *Magellan* system then used computers (on Earth) to combine several successive radar reflections as if they had been sent by and received by a much bigger antenna.

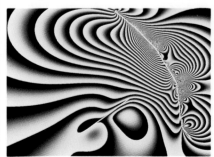

THE MERCURY MYSTERY

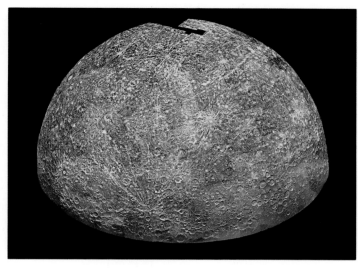
Craters on the surface of Mercury.

The curious way the planet Mercury moves posed a problem for astronomers. It was eventually explained by means of a revolutionary new theory that changed science completely in the 20th century.

Mercury is a difficult planet for astronomers to observe because it is so close to the sun. It orbits a little less than 35 million miles (58 million km) from the sun. The side that faces the sun reaches more than 752°F (400°C). At night Mercury has almost no atmosphere to hold heat around the planet, so the temperature plunges to −274°F (−170°C). No other planet in the solar system experiences such extremes of temperature.

When astronomers looked at Mercury's orbit closely, they found something that at first they could not explain. As a toy gyroscope slows down, instead of standing up straight it leans over and its top starts to move around in a circle. But that is not all. This circle itself moves around unsteadily in another circle. The effect is called precession. Planets precess too.

Mercury circles the sun, but its elliptical orbit also moves around the sun because the planet is pulled by the gravitational attractions of all the other planets. Astronomers understood the principle, but when they calculated the effects of the planets on Mercury's orbit, the result did not agree with what they saw. Mercury's orbit was revolving around the sun faster than could possibly be accounted for by the other planets alone.

The answer to the puzzle came in the form of a remarkable new theory called relativity developed by the German-American scientist Albert Einstein (see page 7). Einstein's theory of relativity predicted, among other things, that a moving object would behave as if it is slightly heavier than it really is. Its kinetic (movement) energy, momentum, and gravity all contribute something to the effect. It seems an extraordinary idea, but when this extra "invisible mass" is added to Mercury's actual mass and all the calculations are done over again, the result does now match the motion of the planet Mercury that astronomers see.

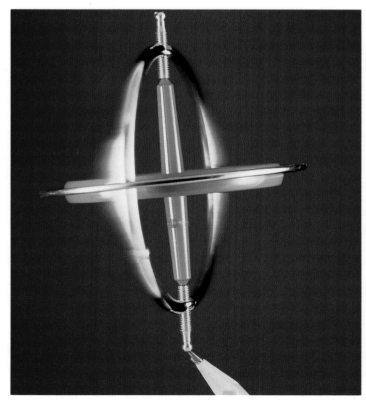
A toy gyroscope spinning.

THE RED PLANET

Mars is a very special planet. For a long time some people have thought it was the home of intelligent beings. But as Mars came under closer examination from telescopes and space-borne instruments, no positive proof of life could be found. Even so, conditions on the planet might support microscopic forms of life. In the 1970s, two automatic laboratories were sent to Mars to look for signs of life.

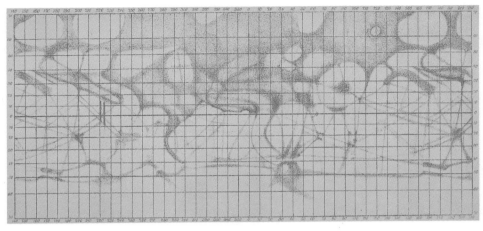

Schiaparelli's map of Mars.

Ever since the Italian astronomer Giovanni Schiaparelli thought he saw a system of canals on the surface of Mars, in 1877, the planet was believed by many people to be the home of an intelligent civilization. The canals were thought to have been built by intelligent beings for the purpose of transporting water from the frozen poles to the rest of the planet. Dark patches could be seen spreading across the planet from time to time as if vegetation had started growing again after the Martian winter.

Some of the important astronomers of the day supported Schiaparelli's view of Mars. One of them, Percival Lowell, produced detailed maps of the canals and the fertile ground that he believed surrounded them. But serious doubts were raised for two reasons. First, Lowell had mistakenly calculated the average temperature on Mars to be similar to the south of England. When the error was corrected, the average temperature on Mars was found to be below zero. It was now more difficult to understand how intelligent beings could survive and how plants could grow in such an intensely cold climate. Secondly, as telescopes improved and showed clearer views of Mars, astronomers could not see the canals. The idea that intelligent beings inhabited the Red Planet was finally laid to rest. However, scientists wondered if simpler and smaller organisms might be able to live on Mars. In the 1970s, a pair of remarkable space probes put these theories to the test.

Percival Lowell, an American astronomer who believed that intelligent life existed on Mars.

Mars appears red because its soil is made from a mixture of clay and iron oxide (which we call rust).

20TH-CENTURY VIKINGS

The meteorology boom of a *Viking* lander. Instruments on the end measure wind speed and direction, and air temperature.

Two *Viking* spacecraft were launched on their way to Mars in 1975, reaching the planet the following year. Each of them had two parts – a lander, which descended to the planet's surface, and an orbiter, which stayed in orbit and relayed data from the lander back to Earth. The landers had a sophisticated automatic laboratory designed to look for life in the Martian soil.

One instrument heated the soil to 932°F (500°C) to vaporize any organic (living) material in it. The vapor was pushed through a long thin tube to separate out the different compounds. These were analyzed to identify the molecules. No organic molecules were found.

A second instrument was designed to look for living organisms that absorb carbon dioxide from the atmosphere. A soil sample was kept in a container with carbon dioxide and a strong light (to encourage photosynthesis) for five days. A detector found signs of carbon dioxide, and to check this exciting result a sample of Martian soil was sterilized. The sterilized soil should not have produced any result in the test, but it did. The experiment could not be said to offer positive evidence of life.

A third instrument looked for evidence of feeding and growth of any organisms in the soil. As soon as liquid food was added to the soil sample, the detector registered carbon dioxide gas, but this did not increase as it would if organisms were growing and multiplying. The *Viking* landers produced some tantalizing test results, but still no positive proof of life on Mars.

THE GAS GIANTS

Jupiter and its moons.

Jupiter's Great Red Spot, bottom left, is a huge storm.

When the solar system was formed, the heaviest elements were pulled in closest to the sun. The four planets closest to the sun – Mercury, Venus, Earth, and Mars – are mostly made from heavy rock and metal. Beyond Mars, the story is very different. The outer planets are made from lighter elements. Two of them are gas giants. One almost became a star.

Jupiter is a massive planet. It contains more matter than all the other planets added together. It is made mostly from hydrogen and helium. These are also the basic constituents of stars. In fact, Jupiter and its 16 moons look a bit like a miniature solar system, but why didn't Jupiter become a star? The answer is mass, or lack of it. Although Jupiter is huge, it is not nearly big enough to create the superhot temperatures in its core that make nuclear fusion begin and turn a ball of gas into a star (see page 9). Jupiter is 318 times the mass of the Earth. The sun is 333,400 times the mass of the Earth. It is unlikely that Jupiter will ever acquire the extra mass it would need to transform it from a planet into a star.

Saturn is almost as big as Jupiter but only a third of its weight. The difference between the two is that the hydrogen in Saturn is less compressed than it is in Jupiter, so there is less of it. With even less mass than Jupiter, Saturn can never become a star either. The surfaces of both of these gas giants are divided into colored bands, mostly red and white. The most distinctive feature on Jupiter is the Great Red Spot. It is a huge storm 180,000 miles (300,000 km) across, first seen 300 years ago. It seems incredible that a storm could last for so long. On Earth, the longest-lived storms are tropical storms or hurricanes that last a few weeks. They usually gather power and speed at sea and blow themselves out as they cross the land. Jupiter has no land, no solid surface to drain energy from the storm. There is no telling how many more years the Great Red Spot will last.

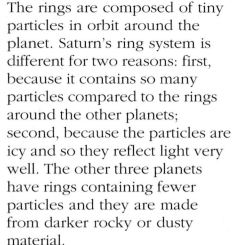

Pioneer spacecraft like this one reached Jupiter and Saturn in the 1970s.

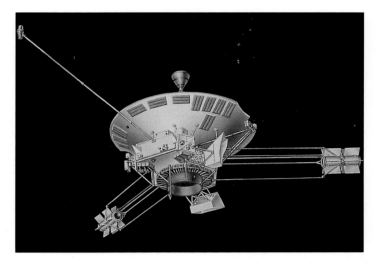

Saturn and its rings (above) and (below) an artist's impression of the particles in orbit.

WHY DO PLANETS HAVE RINGS?

Saturn is very distinctive. Once seen, it could not be mistaken for any other planet because of its beautiful flattened ring system. For thousands of years, astronomers thought that Saturn was the only planet surrounded by rings. But the other gas giant (Jupiter) and two of the other outer planets (Uranus and Neptune) also have ring systems.

The rings are composed of tiny particles in orbit around the planet. Saturn's ring system is different for two reasons: first, because it contains so many particles compared to the rings around the other planets; second, because the particles are icy and so they reflect light very well. The other three planets have rings containing fewer particles and they are made from darker rocky or dusty material.

The *Voyager* space probes that visited Jupiter and Saturn in 1979 and 1981 respectively revealed that Saturn's rings, which appear from Earth to be three or four broad bands, are actually composed of thousands of fine rings. They could have been formed in one of two ways. They could be the remains of a moon that broke up in orbit, or they could be composed of particles left over from the formation of the planet. Whichever is correct, why do the particles form distinct rings instead of spreading out evenly? Scientists believe that the particles form rings because of the action of moons orbiting nearby. If a ring particle orbits the planet more quickly than a nearby moon, it gets a gravitational tug from the moon on each orbit, pulling the particle a little farther out from the planet. As it moves farther away from the planet, it slows down until its orbit is in step with the moon's and it no longer gets its regular gravitational tugs. The moons, called shepherd moons because they round up ring particles like a careful shepherd guiding a flock of sheep, keep the rings in shape.

FLYING ROCKS

The solar system has millions upon millions of chunks of rock flying around inside it. Once, astronomers thought they might be the remains of a shattered planet, but where did they really come from?

Tons of rocky material enter the Earth's atmosphere from space every day. Most rock particles are no bigger than a grain of sand. Friction between the tiny rock and the atmosphere heats the rock until it vaporizes, producing a bright trail called a meteor or shooting star. Larger chunks of rock can penetrate deeper into the atmosphere before they burn up. A rock big enough to reach the Earth's surface is known as a meteorite.

Three types of meteorites are found on Earth – irons, stones, and stony-irons. Irons are made from pure nickel-iron, stones are very like Earth rocks, and stony-irons are a mixture of the two. Stony meteorites contain radioactive materials

A collection of meteorites.

An object thought to weigh about 110,000 tons exploded in the Earth's atmosphere in 1908. The blast flattened over 400 square miles (1,000 sq. km) of forest in Siberia.

A crater formed by a meteorite over 50,000 years ago is still visible in Arizona.

HISTORY SPOTLIGHT

Why did the age of the dinosaurs come to an end? Scientists are still debating a number of theories. Some say that dinosaurs died out when a huge meteorite at least 6 miles (10 km) across struck the earth. The blast threw billions of tons of dust into the atmosphere, enough to blot out the sun for several months and cause worldwide showers of acid rain and fires that covered continents. Some scientists believe a volcanic explosion threw dust and gas into the atmosphere and changed the climate. Others think that dinosaurs lost their habitat as sea levels fell and vast marshy areas dried out.

which decay over billions of years. These give scientists a way of measuring a stony meteorite's age. When the levels of these radioactive materials are measured, most of the stones turn out to be four and a half billion years old – about the same age as the solar system. They are therefore made from material left over from the formation of the solar system.

Some meteorites are much younger. Most of these are identical to moon rocks collected by the *Apollo* astronauts. Scientists believe that these meteorites are pieces of the moon blasted out of its surface by impacts that formed craters. A handful of meteorites were neither as old as the solar system nor did they come from the moon. Scientists finally discovered where they came from by analyzing tiny bubbles of gas trapped inside them. They turned out to be bubbles of Martian atmosphere, identical to the samples taken and analyzed by the *Viking* space probes. These meteorites were probably thrown out of the Martian surface by huge volcanic explosions, and hurled into space.

We can see the effect of a meteorite today in a crater that is about a mile (1.6 km) across in Arizona. This meteorite was a chunk of iron more than 330 feet (100 m) across.

A triceratops skeleton.

DEVIL STARS

The brightest comets look like a star with a fiery tail. In the past people feared them, because they appeared without warning and stayed in the sky for weeks, sometimes months. In 1456 Pope Calixtus III declared a bright comet to be an agent of the devil! Modern science has revealed what they really are.

A Leonid meteor shower.

The first person who successfully predicted the motion of a comet was the scientist Sir Isaac Newton (1642-1727). Newton calculated that comets must have very elongated orbits around the sun and so they are visible from Earth for only a short time. A colleague of Newton's, Edmond Halley (1656-1742), looked back at old reports of comet sightings. He thought comets seen in 1531, 1607, and 1682 could be the same comet, because they seemed to have followed very similar orbits when they appeared. He predicted that if it was a single comet, it should reappear in 1758. The comet did reappear in that year and it was named Halley's Comet in his honor.

Astronomers now think comets are balls of ice and rock that are among the oldest objects in the solar system. As a comet's orbit brings it closer to the sun, some of its icy surface melts and evaporates, producing the glowing head and tail. They glow because of reflected sunlight, not heat. The tail always points away from the sun because of solar radiation blowing against it. A large comet could orbit the sun for thousands of years without dying, losing only a small part of its mass each time it passes the sun. As the surface of the comet melts, particles of dust and crumbs of rock come away too. If the Earth passes through a comet's orbit, the particles burn up in the atmosphere and cause a meteor shower, which can be seen from Earth with the naked eye. There are several well-known meteor showers that occur at the same times each year – the Lyrids on April 21, the Perseids on August 11, the Orionids on October 20, and the Leonids on November 16, to name a few. It is known that the Orionids shower is caused by particles shed by Halley's Comet.

In 1986, six spacecraft were sent by Japan, the United States, Russia, and Europe, to rendezvous in space with Halley's Comet and study it. The European craft *Giotto* made the closest approach to the comet. It had to be specially constructed to survive its journey deep into the comet's dusty atmosphere to within 360 miles (600 km) of the nucleus. A special bumper shield absorbed the energy of

A Comet in Orbit

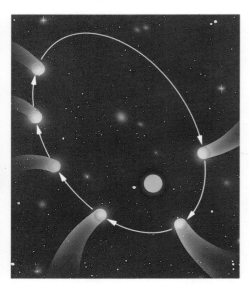

A comet's tail always points directly away from the sun. The tail is a cloud of gas streaming out from the head of the comet.

dust particles before they could damage the instruments behind it. *Giotto* managed to take several spectacular close-up photographs of the nucleus of Halley's Comet. It appears to be a black knobbly chunk of icy rock about five miles (8 km) across and seven miles (11 km) long.

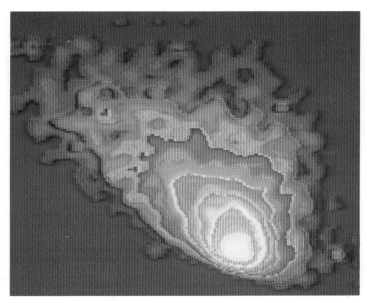

Halley's comet, taken by the *Giotto* spacecraft.

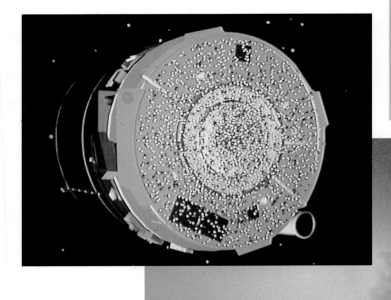

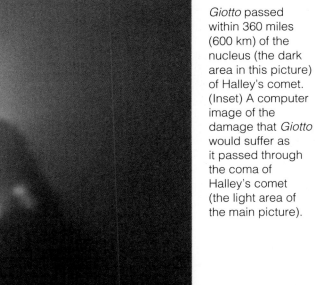

Giotto passed within 360 miles (600 km) of the nucleus (the dark area in this picture) of Halley's comet. (Inset) A computer image of the damage that *Giotto* would suffer as it passed through the coma of Halley's comet (the light area of the main picture).

A Window on the Universe

The Italian scientist Galileo was one of the first people to use a telescope for astronomy. By watching how Venus changed in appearance as it made its way around its orbit, he was able to prove once and for all that the Earth and the other planets really do orbit the sun. Hundreds of years later, astronomers still depend on telescopes to help them study space.

Galileo demonstrating his telescope.

The first telescopes were made with two or more lenses, but the lenses were of poor quality. Instead of focusing all light in the same way, they focused different colors in different places. This made it difficult to make accurate observations. Sir Isaac Newton designed a new type of telescope to solve the problem. It used mirrors instead of lenses to magnify the image. Light bounced off the surfaces of the mirrors instead of passing through imperfect glass lenses. The reflecting telescope worked well. The giant reflecting telescopes that astronomers use today are direct descendants of that first Newtonian reflector.

A weight problem

Bigger telescopes need bigger mirrors, but bigger mirrors cause problems

A model of Newton's telescope and (right) Newton's drawing. His was the first reflecting telescope.

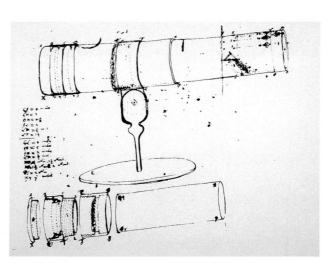

Telescope domes on the dormant Mauna Kea volcano in Hawaii.

that can actually reduce the telescope's ability to focus sharply on faint objects. When a bigger mirror is made for a telescope, it also has to be made thicker to support its weight and stop it from bending or breaking. A massive glass slab stores more heat and cools down more slowly than a smaller thinner mirror. When the dome above a telescope is opened at night, the larger mirror may not have had enough time to lose the heat it absorbed during the day. It warms the air immediately above the mirror and the warm air starts to rise. Cold air then replaces it and this, too, is warmed and rises. The air above the mirror is soon swirling and turbulent, making the image reflected by the mirror shimmer and shake like a desert mirage.

One answer is to use several small thin mirrors instead of one big mirror. The mirrors are steered individually with small motors so that they all reflect their separate images onto precisely the same spot. The Multi-Mirror Telescope (MMT) in Arizona uses six mirrors each 6 feet (1.83 m) across, and together they are equivalent to a single mirror almost 15 feet (4.47 m) across.

In the mid-1990s, the MMT's six mirrors are to be replaced by one mirror 21.33 feet (6.5 m) across. It may seem like a backward step, but this change will double the telescope's "seeing power." In other words, it will be able to see objects twice as faint as before. Scientists have been able to do this because of a new way of producing bigger mirrors that will not make their images shimmer. Although the new mirror is about 3 feet (1 m) thick, it is mostly air! The curved front surface of the mirror is supported by a glass honeycomb behind it. This honeycomb structure is as strong as solid glass but much lighter.

TELESCOPES IN SPACE

The real freedom to look at an object at almost any wavelength the astronomer wished came with the space age. Once instruments were lifted above the atmosphere, they could suddenly see more than ever before. Several countries have now sent space probes up to look at X rays, gamma rays, ultraviolet, and infrared radiation from the universe. Knowing how active nebulae, planets, stars, and galaxies are at different frequencies helps scientists to learn more about them and predict future activity.

ARE WE ALONE?

Does life exist anywhere in the universe apart from on Earth? Scientists have been searching for life elsewhere in the universe for more than 100 years. What are the chances of success?

As the likelihood of intelligent life existing elsewhere in the solar system disappeared, people began to think about the possibility of life existing farther away in the universe. If the canals that Schiaparelli and Lowell thought they had seen on Mars did not actually exist (see page 28) and neither did the beings who were thought to have engineered them, then perhaps we just had to look farther afield to find intelligent beings. There was no point in looking for life on the remaining solar system planets, because, apart from Earth and possibly Mars, all the others were simply too hostile to support life as we know it. But perhaps one of the points of light in the night sky could be a sunlike star with a collection of planets around it. And perhaps beings similar to ourselves had evolved on at least one of them.

An artist's image of an alien spaceship coming in to land on an infertile planet.

The gold-plated record carried into space by *Voyager 2*. It contains greetings in 60 languages, music from all around the world, and countryside sounds.

Instructions to aliens on how to play the record were carried by the spacecraft.

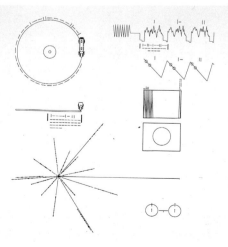

CROSSING OCEANS OF SPACE

How were scientists to make contact with any distant civilizations that do exist? The distances to the stars are measured in light-years. It is not (yet) possible for us to travel to the stars and look for other beings ourselves because the spacecraft we have now are too slow. When the *Apollo II* spacecraft broke free from the Earth's gravity and headed for the moon, it was traveling at about 24,000 mph (40,000 kph). That is the fastest that people have traveled so far. At this speed, it would take a spacecraft more than 150,000 years to travel the 24.7 trillion miles (39.7 trillion km) between us and the closest star, Proxima Centauri. Unmanned probes that space scientists knew would fly out of the solar system toward the stars one day have been given messages to take to any beings who discover them thousands or perhaps millions of years from now. We have sent four spacecraft to the stars – *Pioneers 10* and *11*, and *Voyagers 1* and *2*.

The most practical way to seek out extraterrestrial life is to send something that can travel much faster than spacecraft – radio waves. Radio waves travel at the speed of light – 180,000 miles (300,000 km) per second. They can reach the nearest star in only 4.3 years. There are two ways of using radio to establish contact with beings from another civilization. We can search for radio signals that they might have transmitted or we can transmit our own radio messages

The Araceibo radio telescope sits in a crater in the mountains of Puerto Rico.

out into space, in the hope that someone might receive them and answer.

RADIO SEARCH

On October 12, 1992, the 500th anniversary of Columbus's arrival in the Americas, NASA embarked on its latest project to discover new worlds in space. The agency is spending $100 million over ten years on the most advanced search yet for life elsewhere in the universe. The main dish at the Araceibo radio observatory on the island of Puerto Rico and other radio telescopes that form NASA's Deep Space Network (DSN) will be used to collect more radio signals from space than all other radio telescopes added together. About 800 sunlike stars will be monitored at a billion different radio frequencies. The whole sky will also be swept by the telescopes, but fewer frequencies will be monitored.

THE BIG BANG!

An artist's impression of the big bang, which may have happened about 15 billion years ago.

Scientists have wrestled with the problem of how the universe began for most of this century. There were two main theories. Eventually, one gained more acceptance than the other. But how did scientists know that one was right and the other was wrong?

This century there have been two major theories to explain the origin of the universe. One of them, called the big bang theory, stated that the universe began in a massive explosion at a single point in space about 15 billion years ago. According to the other major theory of the day, called the steady state theory, there was no big bang. The universe

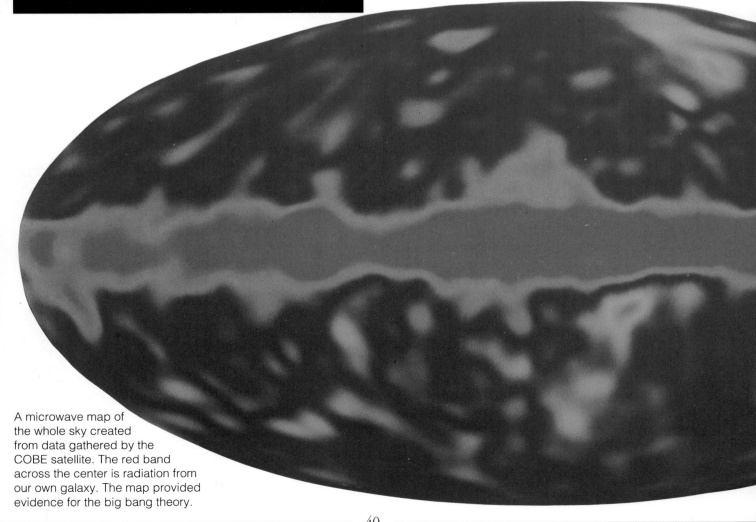

A microwave map of the whole sky created from data gathered by the COBE satellite. The red band across the center is radiation from our own galaxy. The map provided evidence for the big bang theory.

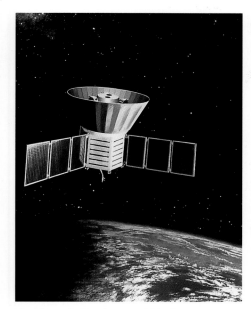

The Cosmic Background Explorer (COBE), the spacecraft that investigated cosmic background radiation.

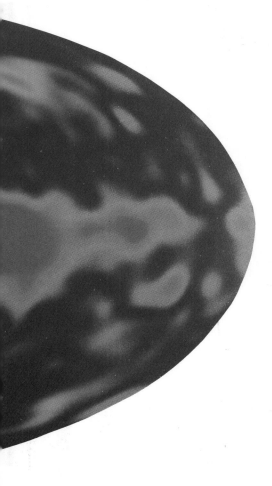

has always existed and always will exist. This theory envisaged a universe in which old galaxies were continually disappearing beyond the farthest that we can see, to be constantly replaced by new galaxies made from matter that spontaneously popped into existence from nothing. Both theories seem equally incredible to the non-scientist, but to scientists the really important question was whether there was any evidence for either of them.

If the steady state theory is correct, then the universe should have looked the same millions of years ago as it looks now. But astronomers have found that the old universe did not look the same as it does now. Galaxies were distributed through space differently in the early universe and there were more quasars then than now. The steady state theory does not appear to be correct. But is the big bang theory any better?

In 1948, scientists calculated that if the universe had indeed begun with an explosion, the radiation from that initial blast should have cooled to about three degrees above absolute zero, the coldest possible temperature -459°F (-270°C). In the 1940s there was no way of detecting this radiation. By the 1960s the technology was available and a team of researchers at Princeton University began the search for the "cosmic background radiation." At the same time, researchers at Bell Laboratories in New Jersey were studying radio signals coming from particular parts of the Milky Way. Their work was hampered by background interference that seemed to be coming from

every direction. It turned out that the interference was actually the cosmic background radiation.

If the steady state theory had been correct, this background radiation would not exist. The big bang theory seems to be correct. Scientists have now traced the beginning of the universe back to 0.01 seconds after the big bang itself. Before then, the temperature of the fireball was so great (more than 100 billion degrees) that our present understanding of how energy and matter behave breaks down.

Although the theory appears to be correct, it still leaves many questions to be answered. One question that can never be answered is what happened before the big bang, because space and time themselves have no meaning at the moment of the big bang. And we can never know the answer to the biggest question of all – why did the universe explode into existence?

HISTORY SPOTLIGHT

The first person who suggested that the universe might have begun in an explosion, a big bang, was the Belgian scientist Georges Lemaître (1894-1966). He thought that everything we see around us now began as a compressed lump of matter that blew apart, shattering into ever-smaller fragments. Eventually the smallest of these fragments became the atoms that everything is made from now. As our knowledge of matter and its relationship with energy advanced, it became clear that Lemaître's explanation was not right, but his basic idea that everything began with the big bang has not been disproved.

THE END OF TIME

W hat does the future hold for the universe? Will it continue expanding forever as it is now? Or will it stop expanding and reach a steady state? Could it even start to contract again? Scientists are trying to predict the future of the universe.

The Hubble Space Telescope is the largest telescope in the world. It weighs 12 tons and is over 43 feet (13 m) in length.

The universe has been expanding ever since the big bang. The galaxies are rushing away from each other because of the force imparted to them by the initial explosion that set the universe in motion. But each planet, star, and galaxy has a force of gravity that tries to pull all the matter in the universe back together again. The two forces are in opposition. Scientists are trying to figure out which of these forces is the more powerful, because the future of the universe depends on it. If the expansion forces are greater, then the universe will continue to expand forever. And as it expands it will cool down. The universe will run down like a

clock to the cold, dark, and lifeless end that awaits it. But if the matter in the universe is dense (thick) enough, gravity might one day be able to overcome the expansion. The universe could stop expanding and actually contract into the reverse of the big bang, the big crunch! That might lead to another big bang and the birth of another universe. The universe might have been swinging from big bang to big crunch to big bang and so on for all time.

The future of the universe hangs on how dense it is. To measure density, you need two figures – mass and volume. Divide mass by volume and you

GRAVITATIONAL LENSES

image A

quasar

galaxy

Earth

image B

The two images of the same distant quasar (above) are produced by gravitational lensing.

This galactic image was taken by the Hubble Space Telescope. The central spot is a nearby galaxy, but the four outer spots are all images of the same distant quasar.

have density. When astronomers estimate the density of matter in the universe, it falls far below the magical figure called the critical density that would stop the universe expanding forever. Could the estimate of density be wildly wrong? Astronomers believe that there may be a lot of matter in the universe that they have not yet found. If there is enough of this "dark matter" it could hold the key to the future of the universe. Some astronomers believe that up to 90 percent of the matter in the universe could be in the form of this dark matter. But how do you find matter that you cannot see? Black holes are invisible, but matter falling into them radiates

energy that we can detect on Earth. In the same way, although astronomers cannot see dark matter, they can look for its effects.

Clouds of dark matter have gravity, so the effect of their gravitational pull on nearby objects should be detectable. There is some evidence that galaxies lying around the outside edge of the Milky Way are behaving as if they are being pulled on by more distant massive objects. None are visible, so the mystery force may be the result of clouds of dark matter around the Milky Way. Einstein's general theory of relativity (see page 7) suggested that gravity might

also bend light rays. And this gave astronomers an idea of how to search for dark matter in deep space between galaxies. If light from a distant but very bright object such as a quasar (see pages 18-19) passes close by a cluster of galaxies containing dark matter, the cluster's force of gravity might be strong enough to bend the light rays. The effect would be to distort or magnify the image of the distant quasar. The effect is known as a gravitational lens.

Studies of these lenses should give astronomers a more accurate picture of how much dark matter there is and help to predict the final fate of the universe.

GLOSSARY

asteroid A chunk of rock in orbit around the sun.

black hole A collapsed star so massive that its gravitational pull is strong enough to stop everything, even light, from escaping.

comet A ball of icy dust and rock left over from the formation of the solar system, in orbit around the sun.

element One of more than 100 simple materials made of atoms of the kind from which everything in the universe is made.

galaxy A cluster of thousands of millions of stars, separated from other galaxies by huge distances.

helium The second lightest element and major constituent of stars after hydrogen.

hydrogen The lightest element and major constituent of stars.

light-year The distance light travels in a year—5.88 trillion miles.

meteor A piece of rock from space which burns up as it ploughs into the atmosphere, making a streak of light in the sky called a shooting star.

meteorite A meteor that is big enough to survive its journey from space down through the atmosphere and fall to the ground.

nebula (nebulae) A smudge of light in the sky that may be a distant galaxy or a cloud of gas where new stars are forming.

neutron star A collapsed star made almost entirely from particles called neutrons.

nuclear fusion The process by which light elements like hydrogen join together to form heavier elements like helium and release light and heat – the powerhouse of stars.

orbit The path followed by a planet, comet, or asteroid around a star or by a satellite around a planet.

planet A large body in orbit around a star.

quasar Quasi-stellar object. An object that looks like a star but is brighter than a whole galaxy of stars.

radio telescope An astronomical telescope designed to pick up radio waves from distant stars and galaxies.

satellite A natural moon or a spacecraft in orbit around a planet.

spectrum (spectra) The result of spreading out a light ray or radio wave into the different wavelengths that make it up. A light spectrum looks like a rainbow of different colors.

sunspot A spotlike area of the sun that looks darker than the rest because it is cooler.

supernova (supernovae) A star that has exploded and temporarily becomes millions of times brighter than the sun.

tokamak A type of nuclear reactor invented in the former Soviet Union to recreate the high temperatures inside the sun and make hydrogen fuse to form helium and release energy.

FURTHER READING

Asimov, Isaac and Giraud, Robert. *The Future in Space.* Gareth Stevens, 1993

Bender, Lionel. *Telescopes.* Franklin Watts, 1991

Berger, Melvin. *Discovering Mars: The Amazing Story of the Red Planet.* Scholastic, 1992

Branley, Franklyn M. *Sun Dogs and Shooting Stars: A Skywatcher's Calendar.* Avon Books, 1993

Corrick, James A. *Mars.* Franklin Watts, 1990

Cosner, Sharon. *Lunar Bases.* Franklin Watts, 1990

Darling, David J. *The Stars: From Birth to Black Holes.* Macmillan, 1987

Docekal, Eileen M. *Sky Detective.* Sterling, 1992

Estalella, Robert. *Our Star: The Sun .* Barron's, 1993

Fraser, Mary A. *One Giant Leap.* H. Holt, 1993

Gallant, Roy A. *The Constellations: How They Came to Be.* Macmillan, 1991

Graham, Ian. *Astronomer.* Franklin Watts, 1991

———— *Space Science,* "Facing the Future" series. Raintree Steck-Vaughn, 1993

Gutsch, William A., Jr. *The Search for Extraterrestrial Life .* Crown Books, 1991.

Jespersen, James and Fitz-Randolph, Jane. *From Quarks to Quasars .* Macmillan, 1987

Lambert, David. *Stars and Planets,* "New View" series. Raintree Steck-Vaughn, 1994

Michael, George. *Galaxies.* Creative Ed., 1993

Muirden, James. *Stars and Planets .* Kingfisher Books, 1993

Ridpath, Ian. *Atlas of Stars and Planets.* Facts on File, 1993

———— *Space.* Franklin Watts, 1991

Vogt, Gregory. *Magellan and the Radar Mapping of Venus.* Millbrook, 1992

INDEX